HAPPY
ABSTRACTS

FEARLESS PAINTING *for* **TRUE BEGINNERS**

Learn to Create Vibrant Canvas Art Stroke-by-Stroke

EttaVee

LEISURE ARTS, INC. • Maumelle, Arkansas

CONTENTS

PAINT A CANVAS

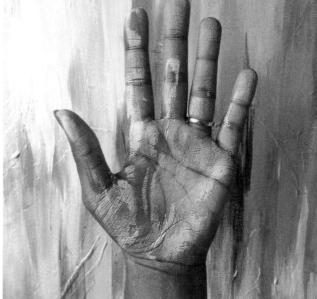

Let's get Creative!

Welcome to Happy Abstract Painting with EttaVee, where I'll teach you how to create bright and uplifting abstract art using expressive brush strokes! I'm absolutely thrilled to have you here and to have a chance to teach you my unique painting style. Everyone has an artist within them and something unique to contribute to the world in an artful way. This guide is for beginners as well as more seasoned painters looking to explore a new painting style. There is no better way to feed your creative soul than by exploring new ways to stretch your mind and creativity!

Why Brush Strokes?

I've been painting brush strokes for about five years and I have found so much happiness in exploring this painting style. Not only are the results gorgeous, but I find the painting process to be therapeutic and uplifting! I encourage you to be loose, free and expressive with your brush strokes. Your natural movements are what's going to make your art feel uniquely yours! Once completed, you will find these colorful paintings add a happy pop of positive energy to your home.

Express yourself & have fun!

Painting abstract art can seem daunting at times, so I encourage you to be patient with yourself! Allow yourself to explore abstract painting with a playful and open mind; knowing that mistakes are welcome. You know, making mistakes can be quite a helpful learning tool. The most important thing is to have fun! Even if the painting doesn't turn out the way you want it to, you can always paint over it and start again!

So light a candle, put on some music and let's get ready to dive into color-filled fun! I would love to see what you create with this guide! Please feel free to share your work-in-progress and finished pieces with me on Instagram by tagging @ettavee and using the hashtag #EVHappyArt. The more you share your work, the more you inspire others to create :)

Merci!!

xo Jessi

Introducing Jessi Raulet

WHAT IS YOUR BIGGEST INSPIRATION?

Nature's color palettes! I love the bright colors of flowers, the lush greens of the jungle and the gorgeous turquoise hues of the sea!

HAVE YOU ALWAYS BEEN AN ARTIST?

Oh yes! I've been making art for as long as I can remember. When I was four, I drew a chalk mural of my favorite movie at the time, The Little Mermaid, at my preschool. The staff was so excited about the drawing that they displayed it in the preschool lobby for a month. My parents recognized my interest and talent in art and got me into art classes right away. Growing up, I dabbled in many different art avenues such as fine art, fashion illustration, photography, ceramics and jewelry making. I later studied graphic design and became an art director which allowed me to mix art and creative strategy!

DO YOU HAVE AN INSTAGRAM CREATIVE CRUSH?

I have many spanning many different areas such as fashion, food and travel. At the moment I'm crushing on new mom @findingpaola. Her feed inspires self-love, confidence, fashion and sophisticated color palettes!

WHAT MUSIC DO YOU LISTEN TO WHILE YOU PAINT?

Ella Fitzgerald's smooth voice is a great painting companion.

WHAT IS THE BEST THING ABOUT LIVING IN PARIS?

The food, wine and architecture! Nothing beats fresh baked baguettes and Paris is known for having the best baguettes in France.

WHAT'S YOUR FAVORITE COLOR?

Deep orange and metallic gold!

WHAT IS YOUR STUDIO LIKE?

My studio is located in my Parisian flat. It's a beautiful room with parquet floors, white walls, high ceilings and great lighting. I have inspiration and current projects on the walls. It overlooks our courtyard where there's a guitarist who often practices with his window open and a DJ on the floor below - I love being surrounded by other artists! However, now that my daughter is getting older I'm starting to move myself out and let her have it all to herself. I'll need to find a new space soon!

WHAT ADVICE WOULD YOU GIVE TO A BEGINNER?

Have fun and be patient with yourself! Explore many different mediums and styles to find what you're naturally inclined to. Oh and make LOTS of art! The more art you make, the stronger your personal style will shine through!

HOW DO YOU HANDLE BEING A "CREATIVE MAMA"?

It may seem cliché, but I make the most of nap time! I really feel it's important to carve out time for art. I love painting with my daughter Savannah around as it's important to me that she sees what passion and dedication looks like. She has already started picking up my paints and paintbrushes and mimicking me painting - so cute!

WHAT'S ONE THING MOST PEOPLE DON'T KNOW ABOUT YOU?

I sing jazz and perform in piano bars from time to time.

WHAT WOULD YOU DO IF YOU WERE NOT AN ARTIST/ PAINTER?

I love telling stories both visually and written, so I'd either be a photographer or a writer.

WHAT IS YOUR FAVORITE FOOD?

I love tomatoes and anything chocolate!

WHAT ADVICE WILL YOU GIVE YOUR DAUGHTER AS SHE GROWS UP?

Find your passion. Nurture that passion. Be confident. Work for yourself. Bet on yourself!

DO YOU HAVE ANY HOBBIES?

I'm learning the ukulele at the moment and am having a blast exploring a new art form!

WHAT IS YOUR FAVORITE TRAVEL DESTINATION?

The South of France by the Mediterranean Sea. This is my happy place as it embodies so much of what brings me joy: gorgeous water, colorful villages, wild tropical flowers, sunny weather and rosé!

WHAT IS YOUR FAVORITE DATE NIGHT?

Since my husband is a pastry chef, we love exploring new restaurants around Paris.

gather your materials

Workstation Needs

- ☐ Butcher paper
- ☐ Water vessel to clean brushes
- ☐ Paper towel/cloth
- ☐ Paint palette
- ☐ Easel (optional)

Painting Needs

- ☐ Canvas (See page 10)
- ☐ Acrylic paints
- ☐ Metallic acrylic paint
- ☐ Soft bristle, synthetic brushes (in various sizes)
- ☐ Fine tip, synthetic brush
- ☐ Paint pens
- ☐ Varnish
- ☐ Gesso

~~~~~~

PAINT

All these canvas projects use acrylic paint, which can be found in the art section of your craft store. Many of these paints are considered "Heavy Body," which means they are thicker and more opaque than other paints. Acrylic paint dries fast, which allows for quick painting sessions. Since it's water-soluble, it's easily manipulated with water. Just about every color you can imagine is available, as well as gleaming metallics.

BRUSHES

You'll only need a few brushes to get started. Use an inexpensive wide, flat brush to apply gesso and varnish. Synthetic bristle brushes are great for creating brush strokes. Look for a Filbert or Oval Wash brush (1" wide or #18), a Filbert brush (10/32" or #10), a Filbert brush (8/32" or #8), and a round brush (#10). You may also want a thin liner brush for some details.

PAINT PENS

Paint pens are wonderful tools for adding fine details and flourishes to your artwork. They're available in many different colors and can be used on varying surfaces such as canvas, paper, metal, plastic, wood and glass. In addition to adding detail, they can also be used to add handwriting to your art. They're available in various tip sizes, making it easier to make fine details or bold marks. For the projects in this guide, I recommend buying white and metallic gold paint pens in various thicknesses. You may also buy any other colors of your choosing!

GOLD LEAF GILDING SHEETS

These metallic gold sheets add touch of shimmer and chicness to the art. These sheets usually come in packs of 10 or more and are to be handled delicately. They can be applied as full sheets, torn apart or cut into smaller pieces. We will use our varnish, which doubles as a binder, to adhere the gold gilding sheets to the canvas.

GESSO

Gesso is a primer similar to white acrylic paint and once applied, creates a strong smooth surface on your raw canvas that is now ready to accept acrylic paint. Most commercially stretched canvas already comes primed. If one were to paint directly on raw canvas without priming with gesso, the paint would soak into the weave of the canvas and you may be able to see the woven texture of the canvas. Gesso can be found near the acrylic paints.

VARNISH

It is essential to use a varnish on your acrylic paintings. It will protect your art from UV rays, discoloration and dust. I find the varnish also makes the colors pop once applied. I personally like to use an acrylic gloss medium varnish gel, but it also is available in matte and satin finishes. Select a multi-purpose varnish that can also be used as a binder.

types of canvas

Pre-primed artist canvases are available in all types of shapes and sizes. Here are some you may find.

4" x 5"	30" x 30"
4" x 12"	4" x 4" hexagon
5" x 5"	8" x 8" triangle
6" x 6"	8" x 10" oval
12" x 12"	7.87" x 7.87" heart
12" x 16"	8" x 8" round

Square

Triangle

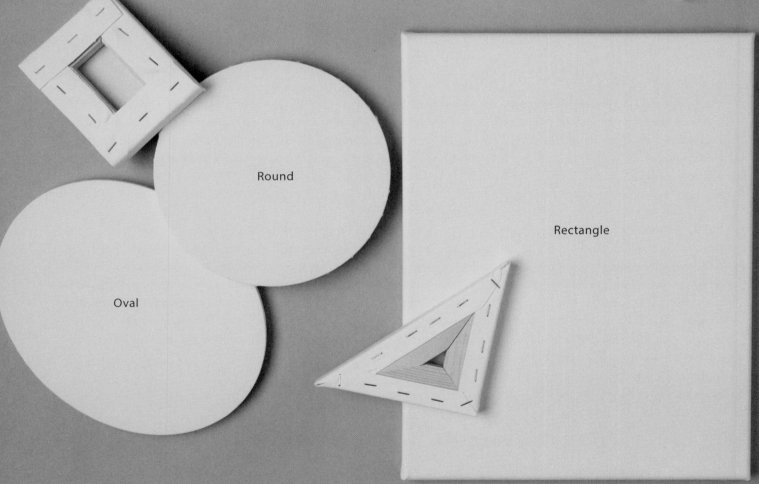

Round

Oval

Rectangle

Canvas Preparation

Most canvases available today are pre-primed and do not need a coat of gesso. Some artists add an extra coat to smooth out the canvas more; it is a personal preference. You'll know it's primed if the canvas is white (gesso) instead of raw beige (not primed).

HOW TO APPLY GESSO
APPLY GESSO HORIZONTALLY
STEP 1: To apply gesso, use an inexpensive, large bristle brush that will give great coverage. Start by painting your first coat, in horizontal strokes, painting from left to right. Let dry.

APPLY GESSO VERTICALLY
STEP 2: Once the first coat dries, add a second coat of gesso in vertical strokes, painting from top to bottom. Painting once horizontally and once vertically will ensure that the gesso covers all surfaces of the canvas. Let dry and your canvas is ready to be painted!

Finishing Your Painting

Upon finishing the painting project, let it dry 30 minutes to an hour depending on how many layers of paint you added. For a clean gallery finish, paint the canvas edges in a matching or coordinating color. Sign your painting either in the front righthand corner or on the back. Once your painting is completely dry, varnish the painting (see below). Your masterpiece is now ready for display!

HOW TO APPLY VARNISH
APPLY VARNISH VERTICALLY
STEP 1: Place the painting on a flat surface; be sure to protect the surface. Next, check to see that your acrylic paint is completely dry before adding varnish. Using a large clean brush, coat the entire painting with the varnish, making sure you cover the entire painting as you apply the varnish from top to bottom.

APPLY 2ND COAT OF VARNISH
STEP 2: Apply a second coat of varnish, again covering the painting from top to bottom. Allow the painting to dry for a couple of hours.

let color lead the way!

Choosing the right colors can make or break your painting! After studying and experimenting with color over the past decade, I have developed a strong eye for building unique color palettes. While I choose my colors intuitively, most of my color choices are rooted in basic color theory. Take a look at the color wheel provided.

PRIMARY

SECONDARY   SECONDARY

COMPLIMENTARY

PRIMARY   PRIMARY

SECONDARY

Quick Color Theory

I'm a strong believer in using complimentary colors (colors that are opposite each other on the color wheel) to achieve balance and harmony in any artwork. It's also a great place to start if you're not sure what colors to use. Start with complimentary colors and then build your palette out from there. Complimentary colors include: Red and Green, Blue and Orange, and Yellow and Purple.

Primary Colors: Colors that cannot be created by mixing other colors.

| red | blue | yellow |

Secondary Colors: Colors resulting from the mixing of two primary colors.

red + blue = purple

blue + yellow = green

yellow + red = orange

Tertiary Colors: Colors resulting from the mixing of one primary color and one secondary color.

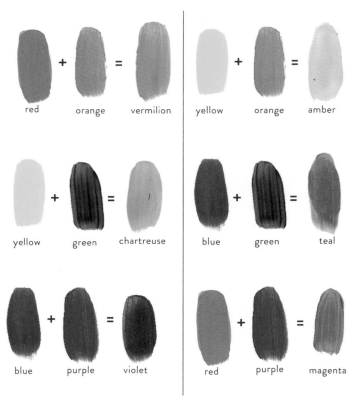

red + orange = vermilion   yellow + orange = amber

yellow + green = chartreuse   blue + green = teal

blue + purple = violet   red + purple = magenta

host a paint party

What better way to spend an afternoon or evening than by hosting a Paint Party
with your friends? Invite your besties over to share ideas, chat, sip a bit of wine,
and paint a colorful abstract canvas.

Here are some quick tips for hosting a happy paint party!

TIP 1 INVITE YOUR FRIENDS

Keep the party size to about 6 people so that everyone
can share in each other's creativity. You can send out
invitations via regular postal service, send out electronic
invites (email, social media or text) or even make an
old-fashioned phone call. If you send out invitations,
make them bright and colorful to set the creative mood.
Be sure to ask people to bring any favorite paintbrushes
they may have.

TIP 2 GATHER THE MATERIALS

Have fun setting up the work area and make it special for
your friends – corral paints in cute totes, use vintage mugs
to hold paintbrushes, wrap a pretty ribbon around each
canvas – you don't have to spend a lot of money, just add
little touches to make the event memorable and personal.
Each person will need a work station, complete with a
gessoed canvas, paintbrushes, acrylic paints, metallic
acrylic paints, paint pens, a water vessel and some paper
towels. Cover the work surfaces with butcher paper.

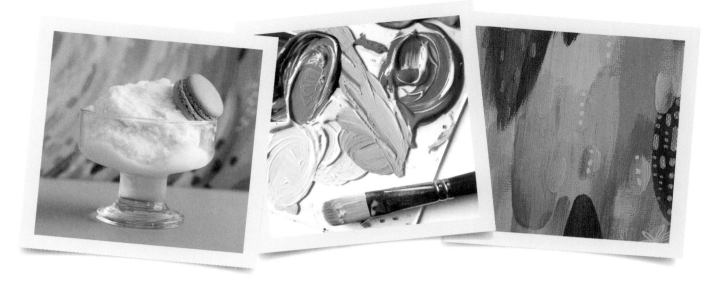

TIP 3 **PLAN ON SNACKS**
Simple finger foods that aren't messy or greasy are your best options. Wine, specialty soda and sparkling water are good choices for beverages. Colorful paper plates and disposable wine glasses make clean-up a snap.

TIP 4 **SNAP PICS OF THE CREATIVITY**
Before everyone leaves, snap a few pictures of each artist with her painting. You'll also want to take some shots during the party to post online or send to everyone. Send each guest home with a paintbrush and a small jar of varnish to seal the painting at home.

bright brush strokes

Layering many colors creates a painted canvas that is vibrant and full of life. Metallic gold and stark white details add that special "oomph!"

Materials

- ☐ 12" x 12" Canvas

- ☐ Acrylic paints (titanium white and colors below)

- ☐ Paint pen (white)

- ☐ Soft bristle, synthetic brushes (oval wash or size 18 filbert, size 10 round, size 10 flat)

- ☐ Paint palette

- ☐ Paper towel or cloth

- ☐ Water to clean brushes

Acrylic Paint Colors

| navy | ultramarine | turquoise | yellow | lime green | light blue | peach | red |

| fluorescent pink | pink | deep orange | magenta | yellow orange | off white | metallic gold |

Prepare your workstation in a clean space. Prime your canvas with gesso if needed.

APPLYING FIRST COLOR AS A BRUSH STROKE WASH

STEP 1: We're going to start by creating a soft guide for our composition as our background layer. First, dip your oval wash brush in water and select a color (I chose pink), adding a little bit to your brush. Softly brush the water-y paint onto the canvas in a downward motion. Please note: The more water you use, the more washed out the paint becomes.

APPLYING SECOND COLOR

STEP 2: Next, choose a second color you'd like to add (I chose yellow). Using less water than in step 1, apply the new paint color, in a downward motion, in a few of the empty spaces between color one brush strokes. Make sure to slightly overlap the colors for a layered look.

ADDING IN THIRD COLOR OF BRUSH STROKES

STEP 3: Select a third color (I chose lime green) and apply it in a few of the empty canvas spaces.

ADDING IN A FOURTH AND FIFTH COLOR OF BRUSH STROKES

STEP 4: Fill in the remaining blank canvas with a fourth and fifth color (I used turquoise and deep orange) until there is no empty canvas showing.

ADDING DARK COLORS FOR CONTRAST

STEP 5: Select a rich color, such as red, and apply it to the canvas to add richness. Next, select a dark color, such as navy, and apply it to the canvas to add contrast.

ADDING VIBRANCY

STEP 6: Select a vibrant shade of the dark color from the Step 5 and use the round brush to apply it on top of the darker color, allowing parts of the dark color to show underneath. I applied ultramarine over the navy.

ADDING PATTERNS AND SHORT BRUSH STROKE FLOURISHES

STEP 7: Using various colors and the round brush, add groupings of short brush strokes and flourishes in areas that feel like they are lacking in movement.

ADDING METALLIC GOLD PAINT

STEP 8: Take the small brush and use metallic gold paint to add more flourishes to the painting.

TIP: Place metallic paint on top of darker colors for more pop.

ADDING FINE DETAILS

STEP 9: Using the white paint pen, add fine details and patterns, such as stripes and dots in areas in need of some excitement.

Be Creative!

Make your mark!
Explore painting with large, confident and splashy brush strokes.

PROJECT ONE: AT A GLANCE

Prepare your workstation in a clean space. Prime your canvas with gesso if needed.

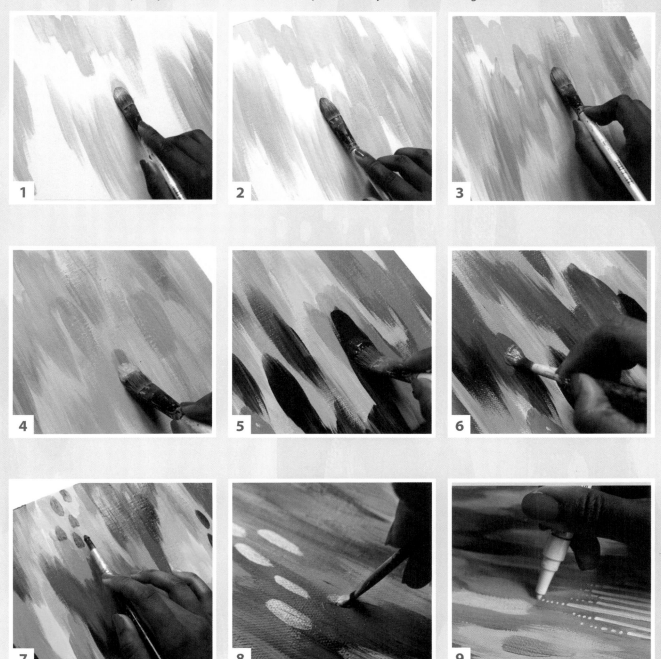

OR
lead the
WAY!

expressive abstract sky

Let nature be your muse as she paints a beautiful and changing sky every day. Awaken your creativity as you look to the heavens and explore a new color palette.

Materials

- ☐ 12" x 16" canvas
- ☐ Acrylic paints (titanium white and colors below)
- ☐ Paint pen (white)
- ☐ Soft bristle, synthetic brushes (oval wash or size 18 filbert, size 10 round, size 10 flat)
- ☐ Paint palette
- ☐ Paper towel or cloth
- ☐ Water to clean brushes

Acrylic Paint Colors

navy   ultramarine   turquoise   yellow   sky blue   light blue   peach

purple   fluorescent pink   pink   deep orange   magenta   yellow orange   off white   metallic gold

Prepare your workstation in a clean space. Prime your canvas with gesso if needed.

APPLYING INITIAL COLOR WASH

STEP 1: For the background layer, we're going to start by creating a color wash, to create a guide for our composition. Begin with putting white paint on the oval wash brush, dip in water and apply to the canvas in an upward swooping motion. Please note: The more water you use, the more washed out the paint becomes.

ADDING COLOR

STEP 2: Take a light color of your choice (I chose pink) and apply it to the canvas using the same color wash technique as in Step 1.

ADDING VARIOUS SHADES OF COLOR

STEP 3: Continue with different shades of your chosen color (in my case, pink) until you get to the bottom of the canvas. Using a wet brush, blend the different shades together. Let dry.

ADDING DARK COLOR TO BOTTOM

STEP 4: Once dry, add darker paint colors to the bottom half of the piece. Blend together. Your entire piece should be smooth, well blended and look ombréd, fading from light to dark.

ADDING MID-GROUND STROKES

STEP 5: Now we're going to begin on the mid-ground. Select a light color from the top section of the painting (I used deep orange, which coordinated with the pinks) and using a dry brush, apply bold brush strokes in an upward-sweeping motion. Next, take a wet brush and blend the edges of the bold stroke into the background.

BRINGING IN CONTRAST

STEP 6: Next, add shorter groupings of brush strokes throughout the painting. Use contrasting colors that will pop against the other colors (refer to the color wheel on page 13). I used sky blue and turquoise.

ADDING SMALLER COLORFUL FLOURISHES

STEP 7: Next, use the round brush to add small groupings of flourishes throughout the painting in various colors. I used yellow orange, fluorescent pink, magenta and navy. This adds movement to the painting.

ADDING METALLIC GOLD DETAILING

STEP 8: Use the round brush to apply the metallic gold paint. Paint along the shape of the larger brush strokes. The gold especially pops against the darker colors, such as navy.

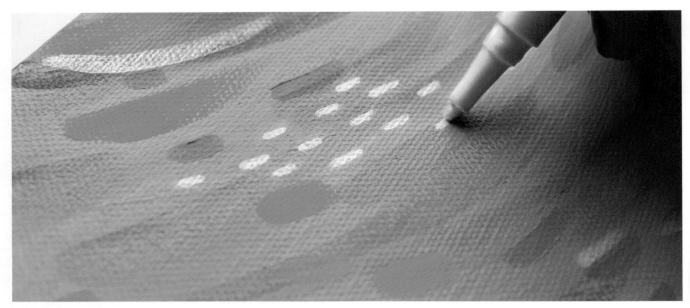

ADDING FINE DETAILING

STEP 9: Add fine details and small patterns with your
white paint pen. Apply these fine details to any part of the
painting that feels empty or needs visual movement to
help the eye dance around the painting.

Be Creative!

Take a walk outside and admire the beautiful
colors found in the sky. Study the vibrant
colors in sunrises, sunsets and at twilight in
real life and in photos. Also, notice how those
colors look on reflective surfaces such as water
and glass windows. Use this inspiration to bring
your abstract sky to life.

PROJECT TWO: AT A GLANCE

Prepare your workstation in a clean space. Prime your canvas with gesso if needed.

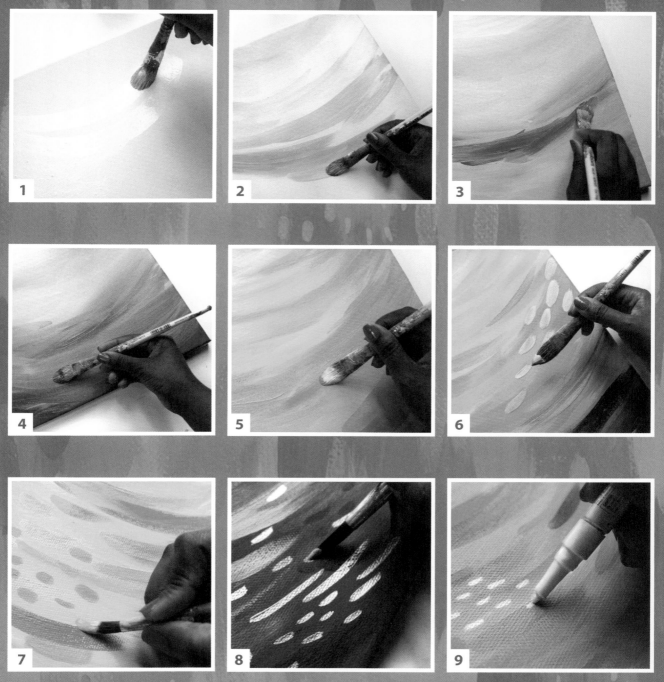

MAKE
your

art heart

Love is in the air and on the canvas! Bright, whimsical colors pair with metallic gold for a heart-stopping work of art.

Materials

- ☐ 12" x 12" canvas

- ☐ Acrylic paints (titanium white and colors below)

- ☐ Paint pens (white, gold metallic)

- ☐ 3" wide synthetic bristle all-purpose brush

- ☐ Soft bristle, synthetic brushes (oval wash or size 18 filbert, size 10 round, size 10 flat)

- ☐ Paint palette

- ☐ Paper towel or cloth

- ☐ Water to clean brushes

Acrylic Paint Colors

navy   turquoise   light blue   lime green   pale pink

fluorescent pink   pink   deep orange   magenta

Prepare your workstation in a clean space. Prime your canvas with gesso if needed.

PAINTING BACKGROUND

STEP 1: Start by painting the background of your canvas a solid color of your choice (I chose pink), using the 3" wide brush. Make sure to use at least two coats, so the background is smooth and opaque.

CREATING BACKGROUND PATTERN

STEP 2: Select the round brush and using a second color of your choice, create a simple pattern on the background. Think polka dots or stripes. I used pale pink.

HEART OUTLINE

STEP 3: Paint a heart outline in the center of your canvas. I used lime green.

FILL IN HEART

STEP 4: Next select a base color (I chose light blue) for your heart and fill in the outline using the oval wash brush.

PAINTING BRUSH STROKES

STEP 5: Start painting brush strokes inside of the heart with the flat brush. You'll want to make sure you paint along the shape of the heart. This will keep all of your brush strokes in the same direction. Begin building up your brush strokes with many colors. I started with pale pink.

BUILD UP LAYERS AND COLORS

STEP 6: Using different colors, continue to build up brush, stroke layers along the shape of the heart. I chose deep orange, turquoise, magenta and lime green.

ADDING DARKER COLORS

STEP 7: Add darker hues for contrast, such as navy and fluorescent pink.

PAINT PEN DETAILING

STEP 8: Using the white paint pen, begin adding fine details inside the brush strokes.

METALLIC GOLD DETAILING

STEP 9: Add some shimmer by adding fine details using the gold metallic paint pen.

Be Creative!

Try painting with your non-dominant hand to challenge yourself and give your heart some added expression.

PROJECT THREE: AT A GLANCE

Prepare your workstation in a clean space. Prime your canvas with gesso if needed.

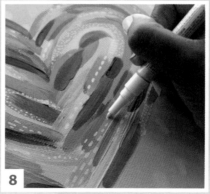

Stay BRIGHT

multi canvas strokes

What's better than one brush stroke canvas? Why, nine brush stroke canvases of course! By taping the small canvases together and painting them as one, you'll have a great work of art in no time.

Materials

- ☐ Nine 5" x 5" canvases (This project can be done using as many or as few canvases as you wish.)

- ☐ Acrylic paints (titanium white and colors below)

- ☐ Paint pen (white, gold metallic)

- ☐ Soft bristle, synthetic brushes (oval wash or size 18 filbert, size 10 round)

- ☐ Masking tape

- ☐ Paint palette

- ☐ Paper towel or cloth

- ☐ Water to clean brushes

Acrylic Paint Colors

phthalo green   navy   ultramarine   turquoise   yellow   lime green   light blue

fluorescent pink   pink   deep orange   magenta   metallic gold

TAPING CANVASES

STEP 1: Begin by bringing all of the canvases together into one big canvas. Once you've arranged your canvases, turn them over so they are canvas-side down. Tape them together using masking tape. I used three pieces of tape horizontally and three pieces of tape vertically. This way the canvases will hold together as you paint.

PAINTING FIRST BACKGROUND LAYER

STEP 2: Flip your taped canvases canvas-side up. We're going to start by creating a soft guide for our composition as our background layer. First, dip your oval wash brush in water and select a color (I chose phthalo green); add a little bit of paint to your brush. Softly brush the water-y paint onto the canvas in a downward motion. Please note: The more water you use, the more washed out the paint becomes.

ADDING IN SECOND AND THIRD COLOR OF BRUSH STROKES

STEP 3: Select a second and third color (I used lime green and deep orange) and apply them to some of the blank canvas space, building up the colorful layers until there is no more blank canvas space left. Be sure to overlap the colors a bit.

PAINTING IN THE CREVICES

STEP 4: Start incorporating darker colors with the round brush for contrast; I used navy, ultramarine, fluorescent pink and pink. Paint the areas between the canvases, where the brush stroke starts on one canvas and ends on another.

BUILDING LAYERS OF COLOR

STEP 5: Continue to build up the colors until you're happy with the outcome.

ADDING FLOURISHES

STEP 6: Use the flat brush to add brush stroke flourishes in areas that feel flat. I used light blue to liven things up.

ADDING GOLD FLOURISHES

STEP 7: Use metallic gold paint, go through and add flourishes throughout the painting. Add the metallic brush strokes on top of darker colors, so that they pop better!

ADDING FINE GOLD DETAILS

STEP 8: Using the metallic gold paint pen, add small fine details, such as tiny dots, on top of the darker brush strokes.

ADDING FINE WHITE DETAILS

STEP 9: Using the white paint pen, add small fine details throughout the painting. To prevent the canvases from sticking together, remove the tape on the back, separate the canvases and allow them to dry separately.

Be Creative!

It's fun to look at abstract art from many different angles. Turn your grouped canvases and try painting upside down.

Prepare your workstation in a clean space. Prime your canvas with gesso if needed.

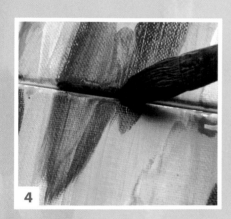

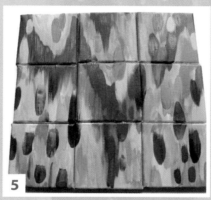

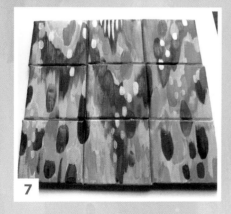

make time

FOR Art

monochromatic glam

A monochromatic painting is a piece of art made of various shades, tones and tints of one color. Think about what color you would like to explore! I experimented with blue and all its variations and subtleties.

Materials

- ☐ 30" x 30" canvas

- ☐ Acrylic paints (titanium white and colors below)

- ☐ Gloss varnish (to use as a binder and as a finish)

- ☐ A pack of gold leaf sheets, containing at least 10 sheets

- ☐ Soft bristle, synthetic brushes (oval wash or size 18 filbert, size 10 round, size 6 round)

- ☐ Paint palette

- ☐ Paper towel or cloth

- ☐ Water to clean brushes

Acrylic Paint Colors

navy   ultramarine   turquoise   sky blue   light blue

magenta   purple   lilac   metallic gold

Prepare your workstation in a clean space. Prime your canvas with gesso if needed.

PAINTING BACKGROUND AND FIRST LAYER

STEP 1: Begin by painting a solid background in a bright color (I chose sky blue) of your choice. Next, select a darker shade (ultramarine for me) and begin lightly painting your first layer. This is where you'll create the general shape of the composition. I chose a zigzag or chevron composition.

PAINTING LAYERS TWO AND THREE

STEP 2: Select the darkest shade of your chosen color (I chose navy) and apply bold brush strokes along the guide you created in Step 1. Select a lighter tint of your color (I used light blue) and paint around the darker brush strokes, slightly overlapping them.

PAINTING LAYER FOUR

STEP 3: Next we will paint a fourth color in between the existing brush strokes. This color can be slightly different in order to add a break for the eye; I used purple. After adding the fourth shade of color, select any shade and blend the areas between the colors together using a wet paintbrush. The idea is to create a merging color effect.

ADDING BINDER

STEP 4: Time to add the gold leaf sheets! Once the surface of the canvas is dry, use the acrylic binder (the varnish) to cover the bottom third of the canvas.

BEGIN ADDING GOLD LEAF SHEETS

STEP 5: While the varnish binder is still wet, take your first gold leaf sheet and remove it from the protective paper. Slowly place the gold leaf sheet onto the canvas and smooth gently.

GOLD LEAF PLACED

STEP 6: Continue adding gold leaf sheets across the bottom of the canvas until it is covered in gold leaf.

OVERLAPPING THE GOLD SHEET

STEP 7: Move back up to the upper brush stroke area of the painting and continue to build this area with more brush stroke layers using various shades of your chosen color. Make sure to overlap the gold areas a bit with the brush strokes; this gives the illusion that the brush strokes are trickling over the gold leaf.

ADDING FLOURISHES

STEP 8: Once you are happy with how the brush strokes look, use the larger round brush to add flourishes in areas that appear to be flat or lacking movement. Alternate between using colors from your palette and metallic gold paint.

ADDING FINE DETAILS.

STEP 9: Using the smaller round brush and a light shade, add fine detailing in areas that feel flat.

Be Creative!

Since we're creating a monochromatic painting based on one color, focus on creating interesting shapes and forms.

PROJECT FIVE: AT A GLANCE

Prepare your workstation in a clean space. Prime your canvas with gesso if needed.

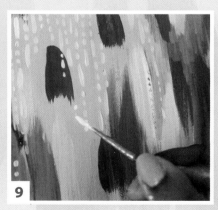

Create
MORE

THAN YOU CONSUME

artful paper

Explore mixed media painting with decorative paper. Choose a paper (or two) that speaks to you both in subject matter and color.

Materials

☐ 12" x 12" canvas

☐ Acrylic paints (titanium white and colors below)

☐ Paint pen (metallic gold)

☐ Gloss varnish

☐ Decoupage paper

☐ Soft bristle, synthetic brushes (oval wash or size 18 filbert, size 10 round, size 10 flat)

☐ 3" wide synthetic bristle all purpose brush

☐ Paint palette

☐ Paper towel or cloth

☐ Water to clean brushes

Acrylic Paint Colors

phthalo green   yellow   lime green   light blue   peach   red

fluorescent pink   pink   deep purple   lilac   off white   metallic gold

Prepare your workstation in a clean space. Prime your canvas with gesso if needed.

PAINT BASE

STEP 1: Use the wide all purpose brush to paint background a solid color. I recommend using two coats; I chose yellow. While the background layer dries, decide where on the canvas you'd like to add your sheet of decorative paper and tear the paper into the desired shape(s).

TIP: Tear paper for a hand torn look and cut paper with scissors for clean lines. I prefer to tear the paper as I find it adds a touch of humanity into the finished piece.

APPLYING BINDER

STEP 2: Once the surface of the canvas is dry, take your varnish, which also doubles as a binder, and use the oval wash brush to cover the areas of the painting where you would like to add the decorative paper.

APPLYING PAPER

STEP 3: Place the decorative paper shape on the binder and smooth gently. Continue adding decorative paper in the areas where binder has been added. Wrap any excess paper to canvas back and trim as necessary.

SEALING PAPER

STEP 4: Once all of your paper is in place, use the oval wash brush to apply varnish on top of the decorative paper, sealing it onto the canvas.

BRUSH STROKE LAYER

STEP 5: Using various colors, begin painting brush strokes on the bottom half of the painting. Be sure to slightly overlap the brush strokes with the decorative paper to give the effect that the brush strokes are flowing over the paper. I used lilac, light blue, pink and fluorescent pink brush strokes.

ADD LIGHTER COLOR

STEP 6: Keep building up the colors (such as deep purple, red and phthalo green) on the bottom. Take a lighter paint color, like off white, and paint the top half of the painting.

OVERLAPPING BRUSH STROKES

STEP 7: Add overlapping brush strokes to the painting, making sure to use some of the colors from the decorative paper for a more harmonious look. I added lime green.

ADDING GOLD DETAILING

STEP 8: Using a smaller brush of your choice, add metallic gold paint throughout the painting.

ADDING FINE GOLD DETAILING

STEP 9: Using the metallic gold paint pen, add fine gold detailing inside the darker brush stroked areas.

Be Creative!

Don't be afraid to explore new colors that you would normally shy away from. Create unexpected color combinations by adding three colors you wouldn't think "go" together.

PROJECT SIX: AT A GLANCE

Prepare your workstation in a clean space. Prime your canvas with gesso if needed.

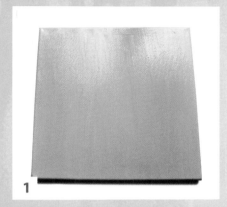

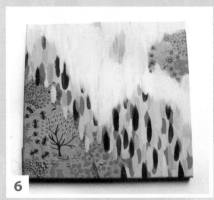

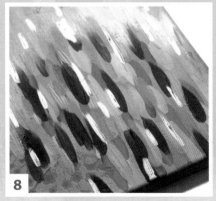

Today is a beautiful DAY to Start

Amazing YOU!

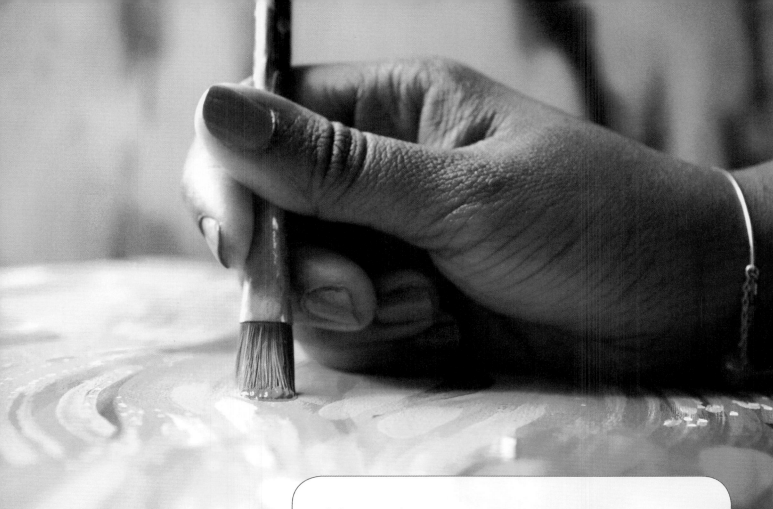

Meet Jessi

Born and raised in Indiana, Jessi began her love affair with color at the age of four and has been creating ever since. She moved to San Francisco where she worked as a art director in advertising for top Bay Area clients. In 2013, she moved to Paris for love where she started creating colorful fine art pieces and designs to brighten up her surroundings. Thus the vibrant world of EttaVee was born!

Jessi is inspired by life in France, travel adventures, tropical settings, colorful fruit and pop culture. Since its launch in 2014, EttaVee has become a lifestyle brand that expresses optimism and joy through color. EttaVee's cheerful designs have been featured on home décor, stationery, tech accessories, textiles and apparel.

every artist was first
an amateur

RALPH WALDO EMERSON

creativity takes courage

HENRI MATISSE

pave your own path and
be fearless

ADAM DRAPER

a picture is a poem
without words

HORACE

creativity is contagious,
pass it on

ALBERT EINSTEIN

time you enjoy wasting
is not wasted time

MARTHE TROLY-CURTIN

do not fear failure but rather
fear not trying

ROY T. BENNETT

be strong, be fearless,
be beautiful

MISTY COPELAND

there are always flowers for
those who want to see them

HENRI MATISSE

painting is easy when you
don't know how, but very
difficult when you do

EDGAR DEGAS